Oliver's Travels

WRITTEN AND ILLUSTRATED BY

Carolyn Seabolt

For information, please contact
Fideli Publishing, Inc.:
info@fidelipublishing.com
www.FideliPublishing.com

This book is dedicated to Oliver,
my Siamese cat.
He is a constant source of entertainment,
and without him this book
would not have happened.

Hi I'm Oliver, a chocolate point Siamese cat. I live in rural Carroll County, Maryland with my sister Roxy. She has a book of her own about her day in the garden outside the studio where we live with our human.

Roxy and I often sit on our human's lap as she looks at photo books and tells us stories about places around the world she has visited. Roxy usually takes a nap after about ten minutes, but I am very interested.

One night as I was curled up on my bed ready for a restful nights sleep, I started to dream about adventures I would have while traveling the world.

I would visit Egypt, Greece, Spain, Italy, Germany, Holland, London and Paris of course.

It was a sunny morning as I said goodbye to my human and sister Roxy and set off for the airport.

I had my ticket, passport, camera and toothbrush. I was ready for my adventure.

I got a great seat on the plane by the window and very
nice seat partners.

After a lovely breakfast, it was time for a nap.

My first stop was Egypt, the land of the pharaohs.

I boarded a tour bus with a lady that explained all about Egypt and its customs.

I saw the Nile River where once crocodiles and hippos swam. Thanks goodness I didn't see a cobra.

The great pyramids at Giza were very large. I got to ride a camel up to them from the bus. I felt like royalty in Egypt since the Egyptians loved and worshipped cats. I have always considered myself royal.

Today I'm off to London. I'll tour the city on one of their red double decker buses. I'll sit on the top level so I can get great photos to share when I get home.

The tour guide will tell me all about Big Ben, the Tower of London, and I will see the changing of the guards at Buckingham Palace. Then I'll go through Picadilly Circus and stop at Harrods Department Store for some quick shopping.

I'll find something nice for Roxy. If I'm lucky maybe I'll get to have afternoon tea with the Queen.

Today's journey takes me to Holland. It should be a more relaxing pace than London. In Holland almost everyone rides a bicycle.

I'll get to rest while sitting in the beautiful tulips that Holland is famous for and watch the windmills turn in the breeze.

This is where Vincent van Gogh and Rembrandt were born, two of the world's most talented artists. Hopefully I'll get to see a museum with their paintings.

I also need to get a piece of Delftware pottery to take home for my human.

I know she is missing me.

Guten Morgen! (good morning). What a beautiful day here in Germany. I'm going for a train ride through the countryside to see castles, and then enjoy some local favorites like sauerbraten and schnitzel, and of course pretzels and beer.

If it was September I could visit the Oktoberfest, but instead I think I will tour one of the many car factories here: BMW, Mercedes or Volkswagen. This is going to be a hard choice.

Bonjour mes amies! I'm in Paris, the "City of Lights."
Today my friend Taffy and I will rent a scooter and tour Paris. We will be going to see the Eiffle Tower where we will enjoy some cheese and a baguette for lunch. Then off to see the Louvre and Versailles and take some photos at Notre Dame Cathedral.

Au revoir!
Goodbye, until we meet again.

Hola, amigo!

Going to take some time today to write a few postcards. I think Aunt Judy would like one of the Andalusian horses, the breed prized by the nobility here in Spain.

I'll send my human a postcard of the street cats in Barcelona. There are so many of them, but none as handsome as me. After a short nap, I'm off to the bullfights, and then a relaxing evening with some classical guitar music and *leche frita* (milk pudding) for dinner.

Tomorrow I'm off to Italy.

Adios!

Postcard

É una bella giornata (it's a beautiful day) here in Italy, a country that looks like a boot surrounded by water. It is so beautiful here and so much to see and do.

I'm going to visit Michelangelo's David, the Leaning Tower of Pisa, the Colosseum, Pantheon and Vatican City, where the Pope lives. I can't wait for Venice, the city built on a lagoon. I'm going to ride in a hand painted Venetian gondola through the canals, looking at the palazza and ancient bridges.

I hope the gondolier will serenade me.

For dinner tonight I'm having spaghetti!

I'm starting to miss my family, but before I go home I have to visit Athens Greece where the first Olympic games began.

I also want to visit the Parthenon and hear some of the stories (mythology) of the Greek gods and goddesses.

I yawn and stretch as the sun rises and the birds begin to sing.

I hear my human pouring food into my bowl for breakfast.

What an adventure I had in my dreams last night. I'm glad to be home in my bed with my family.

Of course, I didn't really take those trips, I'm a cat!

But one can always dream.

Meow!

(The End)

About the Author

I have always dreamed of writing and illustrating children's books.

My dream has become a reality. This is my second book. My first being, *My Day in the Garden*, which I'm holding in the photo to the right.

I have also illustrated books for author Jim Huckleberry. They include:

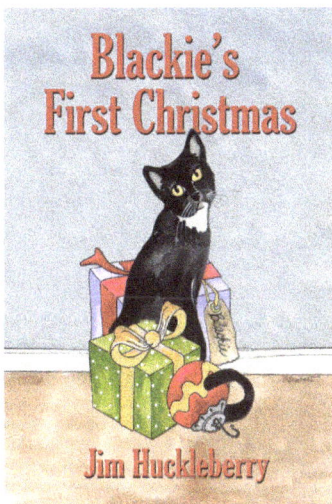

Blackie's First Christmas

The Christmas Cat

Bells are Ringing

www.ingramcontent.com/pod-product-compliance
Lightning Source LLC
Chambersburg PA
CBHW040304100426
42811CB00011B/1356